ACKNOWLEDGMENTS

How it ended up in this format owes much to the erudite discussions held over lunch at York St John University and the wise words of Julian Stern, Tony Leach & Jeff Buckles.

Wellbeing, Vulnerability & Life-chances: A critical introduction for Childhood Studies

Rob Creasy

Copyright © 2020 Rob Creasy

All rights reserved.

ISBN: 9781654413422

DEDICATION

To Fi as always for her contribution and insight.

CONTENTS

    Acknowledgments   i

1. Wellbeing   1
   1.1 What do we mean by wellbeing
   1.2 Wellbeing in context
   1.3 Inequality and wellbeing
   1.4 The key ideas that really should be in an essay

2. Vulnerable Children   12
   2.1 A discourse of children as naturally vulnerable
   2.2 Policy and need
   2.3 Vulnerability in social context
   2.4 What might you use in an essay out of this chapter?

3. Life-chances in an age of inequality   22
   3.1 Life-chances
   3.2 Inequality because of ability
   3.3 Life-choices
   3.4 Inequality
   3.5 Key ideas about life-chances

4. Conclusion: So what?   39
   4.1 This book as an essay
   4.2 Further reading

    References   44

1 WELLBEING

1.1 What do we mean by wellbeing

If you are studying any course linked to childhood or to children and young people you will inevitably come across the concept of wellbeing. Wellbeing has become increasingly important in relation to understanding and working with children and young people. This can be seen in how it forms a major part of a number of policies and services. As well as its importance to practice the issue of wellbeing can be seen within very many academic papers and books, (Moore, 2019, Children's Society, 2018, Bradshaw, 2016, Knight et al., 2014, Taylor, 2011, Ben-Arieh, 2006). However, as is often the case with concepts that you will come across in your studies it is something that tends to be presented as though it is unambiguous. In reality though this is very far from being the case, wellbeing has different facets to it, (Dickerson and Popli, 2018). Wellbeing can mean different things to different people and can be incorporated into practice in quite different ways.

So, when it comes to writing your assignments as a student you will look better informed if you can talk about wellbeing as something that is socially constructed and which is not as clear cut as it sounds. This book will give you a basis from which to question what we mean about wellbeing and it will help you to be more precise in how you write about it. Later, if you end up working with children, young people and families, being able to understand the complexity of wellbeing will help you to be more effective in terms of setting objectives and evaluating your work, and the work of others. For example, Moore (2019) suggests that how we understand wellbeing is dominated by psychology. This might be the case for psychologists but that doesn't mean that everyone who is concerned with wellbeing is focused on psychology and Moore asks the reader to think about this.

As a starting point you might want to think about why we even use the term wellbeing especially as it is something that has not really been in common usage for all that long. It is useful to think about how the term wellbeing came into use to refer to something that differed from a medical view of being well, (La Placa and Knight, 2014). When it comes to childhood this is important because very often children have been seen primarily in terms of their health. This is an opportunity to draw upon some theory. You will inevitably come across Foucault in your studies. You will benefit by getting to grips with his ideas. Foucault introduced the idea of how professional groups look at people as if looking through a lens. He originally talked about the medical gaze, (Foucault, 1989). This means that we are guided by our profession to understand people in terms of that profession. So, medical professionals look at health, educationalists look at education etc.

We can see this in terms of the way in which Health Visitors are charged with assessing a child's development in the early years. What the Health Visitor service does is to remind us that a concern with physical health has often been seen to be of prime importance when it comes to children. When considering child mortality and infant health concerns in previous generations this can be seen as understandable but a focus on health often persists when it is less of an issue to be concerned with. For example when writing about wellbeing in the early years, Roberts (2010) states that "health and happiness are needed to underpin the kind of childhood that is *every* child's right." (p3).

This is the sort of statement that is very difficult to argue with. Most of us wouldn't want to argue with it but as undergraduate students you are expected to be developing a critical understanding of childhood so it is worth looking a little closer at what Roberts is saying here. To begin with we can say that Roberts is locating wellbeing as being a characteristic of good health. At the same time there is the implication that a child who experiences poor health will not therefore experience wellbeing. In stating that this is every child's right Roberts may also be guilty of taking rights for granted. In the book, Children, Families and the State I will consider the ways in which children are very often denied rights.

For a definition of wellbeing that works in relation to children and young people I would refer to Creasy and Corby (2019) and argue for an understanding of wellbeing as individual experience, or what we might call subjective wellbeing. The Children's Society (2018) say the following: "Subjective well-being can be thought of as a positive state of mind in which a person feels good about life as a whole and its constituent parts, such as their relationships with others, the environments that they inhabit and how they see themselves." (p9). Drawing upon subjective wellbeing then provides the scope to adopt a broader way of conceptualising wellbeing. Moore (2019) is also useful in how he links wellbeing to the person.

Establishing a working definition for wellbeing is important because like a good number of concepts within social sciences it is a concept that can be said to be slippery. By slippery I mean that what it means is not always agreed upon or it has no obvious and unambiguous definition. This is obvious when you read studies that are concerned with wellbeing, for example try to read, Fava et al. (2017), Wellard and Secker (2017), Spratt (2016), Ecclestone and Hayes (2009), Sixsmith et al. (2007). The details are in the reference list so paste the titles into your library search box to locate them. You will often come across concepts being used in your studies and must always be careful not just to assume that they are obvious or clear. Always try to grasp just how the concept is being defined in the study that you are reading about. Problems can arise if we present social issues as straightforward because many social issues, such as wellbeing are not straightforward at all, they are complex, and multi-dimensional (Fava et al., 2017, McNaught, 2011).

What is really important to understand then is that wellbeing is not simple. It will not be the same for everyone. Also, wellbeing is not a fixed state. It is not something which individuals should seek to achieve and then forget about. Because wellbeing is multi-dimensional in nature it is always something that is going to be dynamic. It will always be changing in both objective and subjective terms.

1.2 Wellbeing in context

I said above that wellbeing has come to take on an increasing importance within services and practice, see La Placa and Knight (2014) for example. When we think about how services for children and young people are provided then we are drawn into considering the policy context. Policy often seems a bit dry to students and sometimes seems a bit remote from the actual issues regarding childhood and how we might provide for them. If you take a module on policy issues and the focus is on the wording and details of each policy or how it changes from a previous policy it will be dry. What is always much more interesting and useful is to understand why we have the policies that we have and what it is that shapes policy changes. What you always need to keep in mind though is that what, and how, we provide for children and young people is always rooted within policy. This could be at the level of organisations which provide for children such as local authorities or nurseries and it can also be at the level of government. What we can say then is that both policy makers, and practitioners, are bound up with policy.

Previously I said that wellbeing is a rather slippery concept. It is often a concept, or a term even, that is taken for granted as being obvious but which, in reality, is not at all obvious. Consider then that for policymakers, and for practitioners, the fact that wellbeing is a slippery concept could make it very useful. This is because by wellbeing not having a clear and unambiguous definition policy makers and practitioners can find it easier to claim that what they are doing is increasing or enhancing well-being for children and young people. Alongside this, as was stated at the beginning wellbeing is a concept that is difficult to reject. Who wouldn't want to improve wellbeing? This takes us back to issues that were raised earlier though in terms of thinking about who it is that defines what wellbeing is or what is in the best interests of the child.

What we tend to find is that wellbeing comes to represent the aspirations that adults have for children. How children understand wellbeing often gets overlooked, (Anderson and Graham, 2016). With this in mind studies have demonstrated that there are differences between what adults see as important for children's wellbeing and what children may see as being important (Spratt, 2016, Fattore et al., 2007, Sixsmith et al., 2007).

There is some relevance here to the concept of helicopter parenting. The concept of helicopter parenting reflects strong and active involvement in a child's life and, crucially, sees parents making decisions for their children in the belief that this will advantage those children, (Creasy and Corby, 2019). LeMoyne and Buchanan (2011) however, report that wellbeing is reduced in children who experience helicopter parenting as a consequence of the strategies being adopted by these types of parents.

In addition to considering the policy context of wellbeing it is also worth considering a much broader context. This is another example of how we might find it useful to consider wider social forces or conditions when we assess and evaluate matters relating to children, young people and families. It may seem a long time ago now, especially if you are a typical 18 – 22 year old student but in 2008 there was a significant economic downturn. Basically, the global banking system had become increasingly unregulated and this had led banks and other financial institutions to engage in a number of practices which were very risky. In 2008, it all went wrong and this caused some problems for the UK government that was in power as it did for many governments around the world. In the UK in 2010 there was a general election and a new government, the Conservative/Liberal democrat Coalition Government came together to form the government. What is important to note here is that since 1979 the Conservatives have been very critical of providing social services (this is because they go along with neoliberal ideas, neoliberals argue that social services should be provided by private companies not the State) and the financial crash of 2008 provided an opportunity to change policy direction by introducing a series of measures that came to be known as austerity. What austerity politics meant for many people and for the UK as a whole was a cutting back, or scrapping of services, such as Children's Centres and a worsening of family finances, (Lehtonen, 2018, Jupp, 2017, Churchill, 2013).

It was also the case that wages stopped growing and for many people, wages are no higher now than they were in 2008 when inflation is factored in, (ONS, 2018). For example, people working in the public sector such as Education, the NHS and Social Services were restricted to pay rises below the rate of inflation for almost 10 years. At the same time many people now rely on insecure jobs in what has been called the gig economy, (Choonara, 2019, Gross et al., 2018). The economy has changed and the growth of part-time and insecure work for some is also accompanied by under-employment or unemployment for many others.

In some ways this seems to be unrelated to wellbeing but at the beginning I asked you to think about why it is that wellbeing has started to be used so much in recent years. It is possible to take the view that giving greater prominence to the idea of wellbeing can be understood as turning attention away from financial matters and, instead, focusing upon individual experience. This is not to say that wellbeing is not important in its own right, it is, but at the same time it can be seen to have emerged as a concern at the same time that economic conditions for very many people were deteriorating.

So, from a critical perspective what appears to be a concern for wellbeing might be seen as a strategy that is being adopted by a government that is unable to improve economic conditions, or even, has no motivation to do so. If this is the case might we see wellbeing as the re-emergence of an old idea, namely that we might be poor but that doesn't mean that we cannot be happy. There again, this is not something that is without merit. Who wouldn't want to be happy?

1.3 Inequality and wellbeing

Happiness is something that has been considered in recent years, especially against a backdrop of children and young people reporting that they are unhappy with their lives, (Children's Society, 2018). However, it would be wrong to suggest that economic wealth is the key factor with respect to being happy. Happiness is not simply the consequence of being richer, (Layard, 2011). It is difficult to assess happiness and the work of Layard stands out. Instead what tends to be the case is that researchers who are interested in wellbeing consider the extent to which the numbers of children and young people experiencing problems can be assessed. So, although the Children's Society did report that fewer children report that they are happy now it is more useful to consider the rising numbers of children with mental health problems.

This is a good way of also demonstrating that the social lives of children and young people are important. For example, why are increasing numbers of children and young people reporting problems with their mental health. We either have to say that something about children and young people have changed or we consider that something about the lives of children and young people have changed.

This brings us back to a consideration of the social context within which children and young people live and the pressures that they face. One important study which indicates how inequality can impact upon wellbeing or on mental health is by Wilkinson and Pickett (2018). There have been earlier studies which also suggested that inequality was not good for mental health, (James, 2009). This is relevant because the policies introduced by the UK Coalition government from 2010 which were introduced above and referred to as "austerity" has seen a significant increase in the number of children that are experiencing poverty, (Jupp, 2017, Lambie-Mumford and Green, 2017, Tunstill and Willow, 2017, Churchill, 2013). Be careful though, inequality is not in itself a measure of how well off we are. It is a measure of comparison.

So, what Wilkinson and Pickett (2018, 2010) are suggesting is that inequality is a major problem in terms of what it means for society and in terms of what it means for wellbeing. What can also be seen is that those groups who were already the poorest within the UK are those that have experienced the greatest falls in their incomes over the previous 10 years and that this contributes to inequality widening. As children and young people are far more likely to be dependent upon others when it comes to their economic position this inevitably means that their position is weakened. Alongside this it is important to remember that the austerity policies introduced by the Coalition government of 2010 and continued by subsequent Conservative governments have also seen major funding cuts to services which support children, young people and families. For example, the extensive, and successful system of Children's Centres developed under the Labour governments from 1997 – 2010 has now pretty much disappeared, (Ryan, 2019).

So, to start to end this chapter then you might want to consider that wellbeing can be affected by the environment that children and young people grow up in. This idea is at the heart of the ideas put forward by Bronfenbrenner (1979). As such you can say that something such as poverty has an effect upon the material world that children live in. We say material because it is concerned with real things, material things. If you still aren't clear about this think of what we mean when we say that someone is materialistic or ask parents and grandparents just why it is that Madonna claimed to be a material girl!

When we consider the lives of children and young people though we can also see that they are influenced by things that are not real in the way that a warm home is real, or how clothes are real. Children and young people's lives can be shaped by the ideas that people have about them. If clothes are material, then we say that ideas are abstract. Some ideas seem very real because they seem so obvious but what the next chapter will demonstrate is that ideas can be understood as being developed within social contexts. For example, what makes children vulnerable.

1.4 The key ideas that really should be in an essay

OK, so you have read to this point and you have been introduced to a range of ideas that are related to the issue of wellbeing. Some of these ideas were more obvious than others and some will have been easier to understand than others. That's perfectly normal. I still read things and struggle with what is being said. I hope that most of this chapter has been fairly clear though. However, it's alright reading and then thinking you get it; what you then nearly always have to do is to think about what you will do with it. There will be more about how to use this book as part of your assignments in the final chapter, chapter 4, but I will end each chapter before that by picking out some ideas and issues which I would expect to have a place in an assignment about wellbeing. So:

- Wellbeing is something that is socially constructed and although it may sound obvious, it usually isn't. We can say that it is a slippery concept and that it is not a fixed state;

- What we mean by wellbeing has often been dominated by health or by psychology, but a social understanding is just as important because saying wellbeing sets it apart from health. Health is concerned with being well;

- Always look to provide a working definition for your assignment. My approach is to define wellbeing in terms of individual experience, or what we might call subjective wellbeing because this is a broader way of understanding it (Creasy and Corby, 2019). The Children's Society (2018) say the following: "Subjective well-being can be thought of as a positive state of mind in which a person feels good about life as a whole and its constituent parts, such as their relationships with others, the environments that they inhabit and how they see themselves." (p9). You can also link wellbeing to the person (Moore, 2019);

- In respect of children and young people, then very often wellbeing comes to represent the aspirations that adults have for children;

- It is important to consider the social context when looking at wellbeing. For example, inequality can be seen to impact upon wellbeing.

It's not that you would have to follow these in the order listed above but I think that this order makes sense in terms of how you build up an argument. If you end up with the social context then you have scope to bring in other issues that may be relevant to the module or course that you are studying. One thing that is related to this, and which lets me lead into the next chapter, is the idea that some children and young people don't experience wellbeing because they are vulnerable. Of course, that should lead you to ask the question, vulnerable to what? What do we mean by the term vulnerable. Chapter 2 will say more.

2 VULNERABLE CHILDREN

2.1 A discourse of children as naturally vulnerable

It is very common to see discussions about children and young people which associate them with the idea of being vulnerable. Because of this it is often said that there is a discourse of vulnerability that is strongly associated with risk. This can be seen to be linked to debates about wellbeing when it comes to children, (Wellard and Secker, 2017, Turnbull, 2016, Turnbull and Spence, 2011). As such we can say that a discourse of risk has come to shape both practice and policy with children and young people especially in the context of concerns about well-being. A fuller discussion of risk together with ideas about safeguarding are covered in the book, Resilience, Risk and Safeguarding (Creasy, 2020), but what you really need at this stage is an explanation of what is meant by the term discourse because if you are not comfortable with what is meant by discourse then a number of academic arguments and texts will not make as much sense as they could do. For that reason I am going to provide an explanation of discourse. If you are already familiar with it feel free to skip the next two paragraphs.

Discourse comes from the work of Foucault. I mentioned Foucault earlier and said that you must get a feel for Foucault's ideas as they are so important. It is bound up with language in terms of how language shapes meanings, but also how this fits in with a way of understanding the world. So, think of a discourse as a set of ideas which operate as rules. These structure what we can know and understand about anything within society. This has the effect of meaning that we come to see some things as normal and natural but at the same time this makes other things unthinkable.

For example, consider vulnerability. The understanding of all children as naturally vulnerable can be seen to be formed within a particular discourse. As such try to think that children are not naturally vulnerable but come to be vulnerable within the language that we use about them and the way in which this causes us to understand and relate to them in a particular way. A short summary that is relevant to family life is in Nicolson (2014). See the discussion of discourse on pages 70 – 71. Nicolson talks about domestic violence and argues that we can only see domestic violence as a problem if we firstly accept other ideas about relationships. In other words, domestic violence would only not be a problem in a society where it was normal and expected for a husband to beat his wife, because it would be difficult to imagine it as being a problem. So, discourse shapes our understanding of the world and makes things appear natural.

In teaching about discourse I have often used Smith (1998), especially the following short quote, "Discourse constructs the topic. It defines and produces the objects of our knowledge." (p273). What this means is that what we know about something, (such as childhood), exists as part of discourse. This suggests that what we know is not real in itself, it is only real in the way that the language that we use acts to construct reality. It is the way in which language is used which makes something appear real and natural. As an example think about the way in which a discourse of risk makes it hard for parents to allow their children freedom to roam.

So, what we can see is that there is a discourse about children and childhood which presents children and young people as vulnerable, albeit some more than others. In doing this vulnerability often becomes linked to types of needs. So, the idea of children in need comes to be seen as somewhat obvious. That said, needs can be categorised in different ways. This means that we might talk about universal needs, or we might refer to complex or even acute needs. This however is another example of how it is important to establish just what we mean when we use a term because although the term vulnerable will often be drawn upon it is often done so in a way which suggests that it is obvious and unambiguous, (Coram and Coram, 2017).

Because of this we see children and young people being accepted as being naturally vulnerable because of their age or we see children being said to be vulnerable as a consequence of some level of deprivation that they experience. In terms of physical, sexual or emotional abuse we might see that it is easier to identify those children who are vulnerable but very often politicians and commentators refer to vulnerable children and mean children who experience poverty.

As to why some are vulnerable, then it is quite easy for us to point to things which underpin children's vulnerability. Children are smaller and weaker. They are less worldly wise and may not understand situations fully. Because of this children lack power. They are weaker and they are, for the most part, dependent on others. What I want you to think about though is not just about children's smaller size which makes them physically weaker. Similarly, don't just think that their lack of understanding is a sufficient explanation for them being vulnerable, after all, many adults also display a real lack of understanding about many aspects of their lives. Instead, try to think that children, and young people, are vulnerable because adults organise the world, and determine what children can do, in ways which make children more vulnerable.

2.2 Policy and need

I established in the discussion on wellbeing that poverty and inequality are relevant when we seek to understand the lives of children and young people. We could also say that the fact that governments from Elizabethan times have introduced policies which seek to deal with poverty, or to respond to the consequences of poverty for society is evidence that it is important. The issue of need is very relevant to understanding how we provide for people. It seems obvious to state that the types of welfare provided by the State will rest upon an understanding of what people's needs are. At the end of the 1940s the UK, led by a Labour Government set in place a series of policies that came to be referred to as the Welfare State. As with any State system though things do not stay the same forever and the services and support that is provided by the State is and will be, subject to change. This is inevitable really because society changes so what is provided to support society also has to change.

I want you to think though that we might act to construct a discourse about social matters which makes it easier to affect changes that we want to see. For example, around the time of the 2010 general election in the UK politicians started to refer to 'hardworking families', (Cain, 2016). This can be said to act to distinguish these families, families who work hard and do the right thing, from those families who are different. The families that are different are those families who are not working hard. What this does is to set up a situation whereby it becomes easier to gain public support for cutting support to families who are not in work. It draws upon an older discourse within UK policy about deserving and undeserving.

Welfare State policies in the 21st century have seen a move towards the idea of support being targeted. The idea here is that support is aimed at those who need it the most. So, think about the idea of children in need. This means that we can identify children who do need help compared to those who do not and target help to the right children. As an approach it is one which gains a lot of support because it raises questions and ideas about responsibility alongside ideas about who is deserving of support and who needs it.

Wellbeing, Vulnerability & Life-chances

The idea of vulnerability fits easily with this approach if we hear that support is being targeted at those who are most vulnerable. It is difficult to provide an argument against targeting the most vulnerable. What often happens within such discussions though is that poverty comes to be seen as being synonymous with vulnerability. It is then a small step to claim that children and young people who experience poverty are naturally, or inevitably, vulnerable. Remember what I said previously though, about being critical of what you read. You might well accept that children and young people who experience poverty are vulnerable but can you say what they are vulnerable to? Typically it refers to the additional needs that they have or the barriers that such children face which may make them less likely to live healthy, happy, safe lives, or less likely to have successful transitions to adulthood.

The concept of vulnerability is quite firmly embedded in what is written and said about children and young people. Their vulnerability is very much taken for granted. In a society which places so much emphasis upon individuality and individual difference though it does seem to stand out that we find it very easy to accept that all children are vulnerable. Once again I would say that this is another concept that is taken for granted as being somehow obvious and unambiguous. The practice of identifying some individuals and groups as being vulnerable has come to be seen as something that is beyond thinking about, it is something that is natural. But is it? Maybe to answer that a bit more fully we need to consider the social context in which children and young people come to be seen as vulnerable.

2.3 Vulnerability in social context

It may well be the case that when we look at babies and infants we can draw upon ideas about natural vulnerability but this natural vulnerability decreases as children grow. We cannot say that a 17 year old is as vulnerable as they were when they were 17 months but both have no input into many aspects of their lives because of policy and legislation. Policy and legislation of course are created by adults. Look at the criticism that has been directed towards Greta Thunberg because of her public actions seeking action with respect to climate change. It seems obvious that many adults find it easy to belittle Thunberg on the grounds of her age. This is in spite of the fact that there is a lot of scientific evidence to support what she is calling for. At the moment, in the UK, we are all considered to be children until we reach the age of 18 years and this can be used against us.

So, what I want you to consider is that with respect to being considered to be vulnerable although we tend to see the characteristics that groups or individuals possess as the thing that creates vulnerability, for example, living in poverty or having a disability, what we should also be thinking about is how we fit in to relationships with others. So, if we stick to the idea that children are vulnerable because they are children we then have to assess who gets to be defined as a child. My father-in-law left school and went to work at the age of 14, as did many of his peer group. Would he have been considered a child? I left school and went to work at the age of 16. I think I considered myself to be quite independent. I was 15 when I first paid for and went on holiday on my own. A friend and I rented a caravan for 2 weeks instead of starting back at school. This was 1975. There were no mobile phones and my parents didn't have a phone in the house. Would that happen now? If not, why not?

What you might consider then is that social, political and cultural factors combine in ways that shape what it means to be vulnerable, (Brown, 2017, Brotherton and Cronin, 2013). For example, in the UK there is a legal requirement on local authorities to provide services for children deemed "in need" or at "risk of harm". New Zealand is more explicit in having a Vulnerable Children Act. If we think about how this happens within discourses which shape how we understand the world that we live in then we can start to see how children and young people may come to be vulnerable because of more general ideas about their place within society and what is best for them. McNamee (2016) illustrates this with a vignette of a young girl who says herself that she is vulnerable to the actions of her parents but that this is because of the way in which the legal system insist that a child's best place is within their family. In this case it is not the girls age that means that she is vulnerable, it is a more general belief regarding childhood and families.

Although, in the example given above, as detailed in McNamee (2016) the issue is a general social belief in families always being best, we can also see how in recent years there has been a significant belief in the benefits, and need for, providing support to children and young people such as counselling or other forms of therapy. The two things can be seen to fit together. We come to believe that children and young people are vulnerable and this feeds into the belief that they require support so that they may be better able to handle the pressures that are encountered within contemporary society, (Furedi, 2004). What is ironic is that the more that we provide these types of therapeutic interventions then the more that it accepted that children and young people are vulnerable. A comparison of the extent of therapeutic provision within schools, colleges and universities now when compared to, say 50 years ago, is evidence of a growing concern to respond to the problems that children and young people are said to experience, (Ecclestone and Hayes, 2009).

A further consideration in terms of vulnerability and wellbeing though is that if we assume that children and young people are naturally, or inevitably vulnerable then the consequences are that as a society we may act in ways which prevent them from experiencing issues and situations which contribute to developing resilience. This is something that is considered in Resilience, Risk and Safeguarding, (Creasy, 2019). This is reflected to some extent in the term "snowflake generation", adults coming of age in recent years who are said to both lack resilience and be hyper-sensitive. The idea of snowflakes points to a growing concern with children who are becoming more vulnerable and less resilient. Snowflakes are discussed further in Creasy and Corby (2019) and McElwee (2007).

In conclusion then, although it seems obvious to say that vulnerability follows from being weaker or from being dependent on others, it also important to consider how it should always be understood as being shaped within social relationships and within discourse. As such it is more useful to understand vulnerability in terms of social context and not something that is wholly rooted in individual characteristics. For example, think back to what I said about children who experience poverty or deprivation being assumed to be vulnerable. This can be said to link wellbeing with vulnerability. It seems reasonable to suggest that children and young people who are vulnerable are at risk of not enjoying wellbeing. But, if, as I have said, the social context of their lives is important it is therefore pertinent to consider this further. That is why the final chapter in this book considers life-chances.

I would argue that if we are to study the wellbeing and vulnerability of children and young people then it makes sense to consider the social context of their lives and how this impacts upon their life-chances.

2.4 What might you use in an essay out of this chapter?

As with chapter 1 I want to end this chapter by thinking about the key ideas which really should be present in any assignment about vulnerability. After all, most readers will be reading this book to help with their studies. This is not going to be your holiday reading selection, I'm sure. So, let's say that you have an assignment that is either focused on vulnerability or vulnerability comes into it. Your job is to convince the marker that you understand the issues. Developing a clear argument within an assignment does that and to do that there are usually some key issues which are needed. Based on this chapter I think that the key issues about a critical understanding of vulnerability are as follows:

- Children and young people are often seen as being naturally vulnerable but we should question this;

- Vulnerability is not necessarily an individual characteristic, it exists as a product of relationships where some groups have less power than others;

- Vulnerability can be seen as being socially constructed within the way that we understand childhood and how this intersects with the policies that are created to provide for children;

- How we understand vulnerability shapes the ideas that we have about children's and young people's needs, for example vulnerability is often associated with ideas about risk and this leads to children's freedom being restricted to as to safeguard children;

- social, political and cultural factors combine in ways that shape what it means to be vulnerable, for example, children who are seen as experiencing poverty come to be accepted as vulnerable;

Overall then vulnerability is another of those concepts that seems really obvious but once you start to scrape below the surface we can see how it rests on ideas and assumptions which are not as clear cut as we might initially think. Discussing vulnerability in an assignment will often provide you with an opportunity to consider discourse. Although a discussion of discourse is not always necessary you might look stronger if you can talk about it in a way that makes sense. It's always a good idea to drop references in to show that you have read around this. If we think of the ways in which social, political and cultural factors combine to shape what it means to be vulnerable then this also provides scope to explore why it is that children who experience poverty or deprivation are seen as vulnerable and this then gives you an opportunity to consider the material covered in chapter 3 about life-chances.

3 LIFE-CHANCES IN AN AGE OF INEQUALITY

3.1 Life-chances

By this point in the book we have considered the ways in which wellbeing and vulnerability can both be understood in terms of being less clear cut than they are often considered to be and in terms of how they can only really be understood in relation to the social context at any given time. Let us start this chapter though by imagining that it is some time in the future and that you are now, if you aren't already, a parent. If you want you could do the same for yourself especially if you are still a teenager.

Think about your children's future and think about what you would want for them. We often think about a good job, which tends to mean well paid and interesting. We often think about owning a nice house, having a nice car etc. When it comes down to it we often want what we could call a good standard of living for our children, as well as for them to be happy and have economic freedom.

It goes without saying that different jobs are paid at different levels. You will know that some jobs attract high salaries and other jobs attract low salaries. You may also be aware that in recent decades there has been a significant growth in precarious and insecure work in what has been referred to as the gig economy, (Choonara, 2019, O'Sullivan et al., 2019, Gross et al., 2018, Gerrard, 2017). The name gig economy reflects the way in which bands play gigs. These are one-off events rather than regular bookings. So, jobs in the gig economy are one-off jobs characterised by insecurity rather than stability. They are usually based around the idea of self-employment and don't come with benefits such as sick pay or pensions. In addition to this I discussed above how many workers have seen their wages falling in recent decades. But at the same time that wages have fallen for many, the value of welfare benefits in the UK have also fallen. Lots of people are not financially secure.

So, if we consider that employment has changed, many workers have seen wages being pushed down and benefits cut we can ask ourselves what sort of job would we want? This is very relevant when we think about children especially as we often see them in terms of what they will become. Would we want our children to have well paid secure jobs or would we want them to have low paid, insecure jobs? Put like that the answer is obvious. It would be odd to hear anyone say that they would want their children to have low paid, insecure jobs with no benefits. This is where life-chances become relevant.

In studying, or working, with children and families you will often come across ideas and issues related to life-chances, (Calder, 2018). Many workers and politicians will often call for improved life-chances for certain groups of children. One important development in the UK takes us back to the discussion of discourse in respect of how what we understand about the world that we live in is shaped by language. In 2010 the Child Poverty Act came into being. The title of the act suggests that child poverty is something that we should be concerned with. It required governments to measure and report on the extent of child poverty and to explain what was being done to tackle it and reduce it. In 2016 a further Act, the Welfare Reform and Work Act, introduced by the Conservative Government, not only abolished legal targets relating to reducing child poverty and no longer required local authorities to establish poverty reduction strategies, it also changed the name of the 2010 Act in a way that hides, or obscures, poverty.

From 2016, the Child Poverty Act 2010 was renamed the Life Chances Act 2010. The importance of discourse is evident in this renaming. As a consequence of the Welfare Reform and Work Act

2016 the Conservative Government could be said to be no longer concerned with discussing poverty and what this means for children as the focus has shifted from what poverty is to being concerned with who might be at risk of experiencing poverty, (Dickerson and Popli, 2018). Poverty, as an issue, a fact, or a concern, has been removed from discussions. Read Calder (2018) for a good account of what this means for children.

If someone is saying that life-chances need to be improved for some children then you can take this as being an acknowledgement of social inequalities. There would be no need for improving life-chances if we lived in an equal society where everyone had equal chances but the Welfare Reform and Work Act 2016 effectively overlooks what inequalities actually mean for those who experience poverty. We will return to this idea later. The first thing we need to do though to make sense of life-chances is to say what we mean when we use the term.

Life-chances can be defined (simply) as any individual's potential to achieve that which is seen as socially desirable. Life-chances is a sociological term which comes from the work of the early German sociologist, Max Weber (any "A" level sociology book will cover Weber) and is often is used in relation to social mobility and education, e.g. Munro (2019). So, as was said above, we might see owning our own house, or having a good income to be things which are desirable but when we speak of life-chances we are inevitably recognising that not all children have the same opportunities. Some children are faced with obstacles to achieving that which we have considered to be desirable.

Now think about the sorts of things that will make it easier, or harder, for them to achieve these things. Whilst doing this you might also want to reflect upon the fact that there are certain things which provide either an advantage or a disadvantage.

When we speak of life-chances we are specifically referring to social factors which provide advantages for some and disadvantages for others. We are not identifying the cause of differences in individual characteristics. This is not to say that we do not have different characteristics which mean that some of us do better or worse than others. We have to think carefully about this.

3.2 Inequality because of ability

OK, we live in a society that is clearly unequal. This inequality has an impact upon children's lives and it means that some of them are more vulnerable to not achieving wellbeing than others. It means that some of them will not do as well in life as others. But how do we know that this is something that is social in nature rather than because of their individual abilities or talents?

Think of TV programmes such as Britain's Got Talent or The X Factor. How often do you hear it said that as individuals we can do anything if only we want it hard enough, or if only we work hard enough? I guess that you hear this a lot. Watch interviews with football players who have just lost a game and consider how often the loss is explained as being because the other team wanted it more. Is wanting it enough?

I really wanted to play for Sheffield Wednesday. The only problem is that I can't play football good enough to get in a Sunday league pub team. Wanting it is not enough. Wanting something may provide motivation and working hard may help improve our abilities but they aren't enough to explain social inequalities.

For example, you are probably aware that women in the UK do not, on average, earn the same as men. Statistics indicate that women earn around 80% of what men earn. This is important in two ways. Firstly, it is important from the position of fairness. It would be unfair, I would say wrong, to pay two people different rates of pay for doing the same work. In the UK before the introduction of Equal Pay legislation it was perfectly legal to pay a man more for doing the same job as a woman. The first Equal Pay Act in 1970 required that men and women get paid the same rate for the same job but in 1975 equal pay legislation adopted the European Community principle of equal pay for work of equal value). In spite of this legislation women still find that they earn less than men. Secondly, it is important because to get the things that we see as desirable, such as a nice house we usually need money and for most of us, we get money by working.

So, if income is a key factor in achieving what is desirable we should be able to recognise that being female has an impact upon life-chances. This is not about the individual abilities of females it is about being part of the group.

However, being female in the early 21st century is not the same as being female in the early 20th century. We can see that social values about gender have changed and, along with this, legislation has changed which has made life fairer or more equal. This did not just happen of course, many women experienced real hardships, including being jailed for offences which they carried out as part of their fight for equality. What this demonstrates then is that life-chances are not static, they are dynamic. For information upon gender inequalities and how women are trying to tackle inequalities visit the Fawcett Society website at https://www.fawcettsociety.org.uk/.

What you might see then is that life-chances reflect what I tend to call the fault lines of society. That is, those social divisions where being on one side gives an advantage and being on the other side gives a disadvantage. Gender is one of the fault lines. Gender inequalities in the UK are not as bad as they once were but they do still exist. Just think about what was said above, in the 1970s it was still perfectly legal to pay two workers a different wage for doing the same job if one of them was male and the other female.

Similarly, in the 1950s and 60s it was often the case that landlords who rented out rooms within a house of multiple occupation would display signs saying "No Blacks". In the same period it was still possible for men to be imprisoned if they were gay. When the law was changed in 1967 one prominent MP, Roy Hattersley, argued that men should not be imprisoned for their disability! (John and Furnish, 2017). To suggest that being gay is a disability seems ludicrous now but historically being gay could lead to very serious consequences.

So, when we think about life-chances there are some things which are social and which disadvantage groups, not individuals. Personal ability can help but it cannot necessarily overcome discrimination that is experienced because of some characteristic over which you have no control such as your sex, or ethnicity, or sexuality, or the social class that you are born into.

What should be obvious then is that society does not treat everyone equally and because of this some of us find it easier to achieve what is socially desirable than others. However, as has been argued, society is dynamic. Things change constantly and some of these changes improve the situation for some groups. There is still much to do to establish a truly equal society but it is far better to be female, belong to a minority ethnic group, or be gay in 21st century UK society than in the past. This is because social pressures, especially the actions of groups fighting for equal rights, have led to changes in legislation and social policy.

So, when we hear anyone talking about life-chances they are drawing on Weber's idea that in any society that has social divisions and inequality some will find it harder to achieve what is seen as socially desirable and some will find it easier. As a concept life-chances is quite strong. It is effective in making sense of how it is that inequalities persist and why it is harder for some groups to do as well as others in life. There are other explanations though.

3.3 Life-choices

It was said above that a concern with improving life-chances implicitly recognises that society is not equal. More will be said about inequality below but for now we need to accept that

Wellbeing, Vulnerability & Life-chances

inequalities exist in different ways. So, remembering the idea of fault lines in society you might recognise that inequality can be identified as being based upon Social Class, Gender, Ethnicity, Sexuality and Age.

This chapter is concerned with illustrating how life-chances play a part in perpetuating or reinforcing inequalities but in recent decades a similar sounding, but very different, explanation has also been used, life choices. It is important to recognise what is different about these explanations.

The idea behind the life choices explanation is that inequalities do exist but they can be explained as being a consequence of the choices that individuals make throughout their lives. For example, you are reading this because you have chosen to study within Higher Education. We know that having a degree tends to improve your chances of both getting a job and in getting a job with better pay. This means that we would expect that you will be better off than someone without a degree. This is not necessarily the case but in general it is.

As individuals we are always making choices. I haven't always been an academic working within a university. When I decided, at the age of 25 to give up the job that I had so as to study for a degree I had the idea in my mind that this would enable me to get a better job. I made a choice to change my life within the context of knowing that some jobs paid more than others and I do get paid more now when compared to the job I had from 16 – 25. As it happens the job that I had at 25 no longer exists in the UK so I might say that I made the right choice. Looking at it like this life choices seems to work. It seems to be a way of explaining the differences which exist within society. It doesn't.

A good way of demonstrating that life choices is not a sufficient way of explaining social inequalities is to return to the example discussed above and to consider gender and pay. In spite of decades of Equal Pay legislation women's pay in the UK is around 80% of what men get paid. It is not that men and women get a different rate for the same job but that on average, comparing all women with all men, women's pay is less than what men get paid. If life choices were to be a sufficient explanation, then we would have to say that women in general choose jobs which pay less.

The OECD publishes data on the pay gap between men and women in different countries online at https://data.oecd.org/earnwage/gender-wage-gap.htm. The table which they provide shows that gender differences in pay are much higher in some countries compared to others. This is useful because if life choices were a good explanation of inequalities then we are effectively saying that women in some countries such as the UK and the US choose jobs which pay less but that this does not happen in other countries. When we look at it this way, and when we consider that historically it has been possible to pay women less than men then we start to see that there has to be some social factor involved in this. In other words we can identify inequalities but it is very difficult to claim that inequalities are the consequences of individual choices.

Remember also what I said above about "wanting it". In the main, wanting something is not enough to counter the social effects of structural inequalities.

Within the UK in recent years the idea of life-choices fits in with wider debates about choice, potential and widening participation. These debates start by accepting that inequalities exist but provide explanations for inequalities as being based upon children, young people and families not being aspirational, not wanting more, and not making the right choices because of this. In turn this is said to mean that some children do not achieve their potential.

This explanation ignores factors such as Class, Gender, and Ethnicity by providing an explanation which rests upon the idea of individual achievement. This reflects a neoliberal view of society in which individual effort and hard work are what matters when it comes to achievement alongside the idea that we can all overcome adversity if only we work hard enough and want it enough.

As I suggested earlier though, these types of political or ideological ideas are not separate from what happens to us in our everyday lives. This is because ideas shape the sort of social policies which then have an impact upon us. For example, consider how the idea of aspiration fits with policy. This is the idea that as individuals we should all, naturally, want more.

This then gets applied to the issue that when we look at those young people who enter Higher Education there is a clear social class gradient. You are more likely to enter Higher Education if you are from higher social classes and you are much less likely to enter Higher Education if you come from the lowest social classes. Politicians and policymakers then look at this and try to explain why. One response was that those young people who don't enter Higher Education were not aspirational enough. They didn't want something that would improve their lives.

In the policy response to this was the Aimhigher project, 2004 – 2010. The goal of Aimhigher was to see a rise in the numbers of young people from low income families enrolling into Higher Education.

Although the aims of Aimhigher can be seen as valid the language that is used within the programme acts to locate the problem within young people from poorer backgrounds, and does not recognise that there are social factors that impact upon why it is that so many do not do so. If participation in Higher Education is simply down to individual aspiration or motivation we would not see patterns that reflects class in this way.

The ways in which Class, Gender and Ethnicity play a part in educational inequalities are well known, (Reay et al., 2005, Reay et al., 2001, Gillborn and Youdell, 1999) A focus on aspiration though just presents the issue as one of individual character and not as a consequence of structural features within society. As such it seems obvious that social inequalities impact upon children and young people's lives in a number of ways.

3.4 Inequality

By this stage you should be recognising that when we are studying children, young people and families although we may focus upon particular issues such as wellbeing and/or vulnerability as per the first two chapters of this book, in actual fact these things often intersect, or overlap. We have established that life-chances is bound up with the idea that society is not equal. We have also raised the point that very often children who experience poverty at home are automatically assumed to be vulnerable. This is quite typical for undergraduate studies. We focus on one thing and then find out that to really understand it we have to engage with some things which we might not have really thought about to begin with.

So, as an undergraduate student studying children, young people and families it would be worthwhile for you to think about inequality a bit more and to consider if inequality is a problem for society or not. If you have taken "A" level sociology you will have come across the theory of Functionalism. Don't worry if you haven't it's quite straight froward. Functionalist theory says that if something exists in a society then it does so because it has a function. In other words it does something for society.

With this in mind there is an argument then that inequality in terms of income is beneficial because it provides motivation. It gives us something to work for. So, some jobs require more training or education than others, or some jobs are associated with greater responsibilities than others. Because of this, individuals need an incentive to do those jobs. Greater levels of pay provide the incentive and therefore society is not equal. From this perspective you might come to the conclusion that inequality is good. Thinking of the example in the previous section though it does seem odd that young people from the poorest backgrounds are the ones who are less likely to enter Higher Education even though this can be seen as something which will boost earning power. Given what functionalist theory is saying we might ask why these young people are not motivated in the way that the theory suggests.

However, there is a further aspect to this in terms of the extent of inequality. It is one thing to accept that inequalities in pay can provide an incentive to work hard, undertake more training, or take on more responsibilities, but how unequal should the differences be? This is relevant because inequalities relating to income and wealth have a significant impact upon our life-chances. Wilkinson & Pickett (2010) were introduced earlier. They argue that it is not the wealth of a country that is important as much as it is the inequalities within it. The UK is a very wealthy country but it is very unequal when compared to similar countries. What is more, the inequalities are getting wider, (Lyndon, 2019). For example, in spite of the vast wealth within the UK, the numbers of children whose parents rely on foodbanks is high and growing, (Lambie-Mumford and Green, 2017). The problem within the UK then is not the lack of wealth, it is how wealth is distributed. You might find it useful to have a look at the Equality trust website online at https://www.equalitytrust.org.uk/. It will provide you with a lot of information about inequality in the UK.

Let us consider this though in relation to the first two chapters. So, let's think about the potential for children within the UK enjoying wellbeing and let's consider the extent to which the UK provides for those children who can be said to be vulnerable in some way. As was considered above, if we want to understand something such as life-chances it is important to consider the context. In this case we have to consider what it means to live within the UK.

How we can know this is also important, however, the United Nations have a system for monitoring what happens within countries and providing independent and impartial reports on what they find. In November 2018 the United Nations sent what is called a Special Rapporteur to investigate and report on poverty in the UK. This is relevant to understanding life-chances. The summary notes the following:

> "Although the United Kingdom is the world's fifth largest economy, one fifth of its population (14 million people) live in poverty, and 1.5 million of them experienced destitution in 2017. Policies of austerity introduced in 2010 continue largely unabated, despite the tragic social consequences. Close to 40 per cent of children are predicted to be living in poverty by 2021. Food banks have proliferated; homelessness and rough sleeping have increased greatly; tens of thousands of poor families must live in accommodation far from their schools, jobs and community networks; life expectancy is falling for certain groups; and the legal aid system has been decimated. The social safety net has been badly damaged by drastic cuts to local authorities' budgets, which have eliminated many social services, reduced policing services, closed libraries in record numbers, shrunk community and youth centres and sold off public spaces and buildings. The bottom line is that much of the glue that has held British society together since the Second World War has been deliberately removed and replaced with a harsh and uncaring ethos. A booming economy, high employment and a budget surplus have not reversed austerity, a policy pursued more as an ideological than an economic agenda." (Alston, 2019)

So, this gives rise to a question, what are the chances of all children achieving what we would want for them. Do all children have the same chance? What might hold some children back and provide advantages for others? The UN report goes on to state that,

> "After years of progress, child poverty has been rising since 2011–2012, almost entirely in working families. The Equality and Human Rights Commission forecasts

that 1.5 million more children will fall into poverty between 2010 and 2021–2022, bringing the child poverty rate to a shocking 41 per cent. One in 10 girls in the United Kingdom has been unable to afford menstrual products, and many have missed school because of their period. Changes to benefits, and sanctions against parents, have unintended consequences on children and are driving the increase in child poverty. The Child Poverty Action Group found that Child Benefit will have lost 23 per cent of its real value between 2010 and 2020, due to sub-inflationary uprating and the current freeze. And low-paid jobs and stagnant wages have a direct effect on children, with families where two adults earn the minimum wage still falling 11 per cent short of the adequate income needed to raise a child." (p16)

Reading this is rather depressing. What is happening is the outcome of conscious decisions that are being made by politicians. When we read something like this though there is a danger that we think it is not really relevant to us, especially if we are not experiencing poverty or deprivation. Marmot (2015) is useful here. He provides a good way of understanding why inequality is detrimental to society as a whole. Marmot's main concern is with health but the way in which he explains inequalities and the effect of inequality can be used across society as a whole. He does this by referring to inequality as a gradient. Think of a see-saw that is balanced compared to one that is not balanced, one where one end rests on the ground. Your task is to move from one end to the other. On the see-saw that is balanced this is quite easy. Let's say though that one end is fixed so that it is touching the ground. How easy is it for you to get to the other end now that the slope is quite steep?

If we think about this model as being indicative of social life we can start to appreciate what Marmot means when he says that it is the gradient (the angle of the slope) that is important (where the gradient represents the extent of inequalities with greater inequality being a steeper slope). We might all agree that the lives of the poor are not good and recognise that it can be hard for the poor to escape that social position. The steeper the gradient, the harder it is. However, I would argue that this is not the key point that Marmot is making. The key point is that a steeper gradient makes it harder for those who start at the bottom to get halfway up but it also makes it equally difficult for those who start halfway up to rise further also.

The relevance of this to a discussion of life-chances for children is that all children are disadvantaged by a society that is more unequal. By looking at inequalities in this way we are also led towards a consideration of society in which those that experience poverty are not cast as being somehow different because of personal characteristics or individual failings. The poor are not a separate group who are different, they are just those who occupy a particular social position but where it is the structure of society that makes it easier or harder to move out of poverty.

This approach also urges us to conceptualise poverty in social terms. In recent decades there has been a discourse that constructs 'the poor' as a group, or groups, which are 'different' to those who are not poor, the non-poor. The poor are claimed to be separated and distanced from the rest of society by virtue of their own behaviour and difference. Becker (1997) has argued that instead of looking at individuals in terms of poverty it is more useful to consider how poverty is reinforced and reproduced as the cumulative effects of social reactions, social attitudes, institutional structures, and professional practices. This is because these act to "label people with little money and little power as 'different'; which then devalue them, deny them equal opportunities and full citizenship, and punish them for being 'poor'." (p. 159).

To think about what is meant by structural factors Jones (2016) is useful. Read his book entitled "Chavs". Jones offers a good example of how individuals may end up in poverty because of things which happen to them rather than because of their own failings or deficiencies. Jones talks to families in Ashington, in Northumberland and shows how Government policies developed in the 1980s led to the closure of the coal mines which many communities relied upon. This has had a real impact upon many families and has seen many experience poverty.

Now consider the life-chances of children and young people living in an area such as Ashington where their employment opportunities have suddenly changed when compared to their parents or grandparent's generations. Changes in the nature of the labour market and in family structures mean that young people face new risks and challenges when making the transition from education to employment. In today's labour market there is greater demand for a highly trained workforce, while traditional craft apprenticeship routes to employment have declined. Most young people stay on in education or training for longer than their predecessors did but higher qualifications are not the guarantee of a good job that they once were. That said those who do not stay on have fewer opportunities and a more insecure outlook later on in life.

From this we can say that children and young people's family of origin is an important determinant of their future success so what happens to families is important as Jones illustrates. However, for some of the most disadvantaged young people, a problematic family background may be part of their difficulties. It is always important however to distinguish between the problems that a family experiences and the factors which contribute to it. Ridge (2013) writes about what poverty means for children. Rose and McAuley (2019) make good use of what individuals who experience poverty have to say about it, how they came to experience poverty and what it means for them. What is also important is to consider just how many families experience poverty but where parents work, (Hirsch, 2018). There has been a long-standing discourse within the UK of poverty arising from not working. In recent years however in-work poverty has increased significantly in the UK as the value of wages has fallen. If you are writing an assignment on what poverty might mean for children and families these three papers will be very useful.

3.5 Key ideas about life-chances

As with chapters 1 and 2 let's end by thinking about the key issues that were covered in this chapter and which would be reasonably expected to be covered in an assignment relating to life-chances. Life-chances is certainly a term or concept that is used a lot with respect to children and young people and there will probably be a number of times when you can make good use of it in assignments. So, if you get the basics clear in your mind this is something that could be very useful for your studies as a whole. So, what might be needed to provide a good account of life-chances will include the following:

- Life-chances is a sociological concept rooted in the work of Max Weber. It relates to any individual's potential to achieve that which is seen as socially desirable;

- It is a concept which only really works if we accept that society is unequal including the fact that some children have advantages and some face obstacles to being successful in later life;

- Life-chances are shaped by social factors such as Class, Gender and Ethnicity, each of which can lead to discrimination and disadvantage;

- Where life-chances are rooted in social categories such as Class, Gender and Ethnicity a similar sounding concept, life-choices argues that success or failure in life is down to individual choices. This idea is individual in nature whereas life-chances is social. Life-choices is a poor argument.

In discussing life-chances you will probably end up establishing where it comes from and what it means and then focusing on one particular issue which may help or hinder life-chances. It is always a good idea when writing assignments to explain what you mean by a key term or concept and then supporting it with a reference or two. When it comes to referencing one is always good but two or more is always better. This is because two or more not only show that you have read widely it shows that the point you are making is sound. So, to lead into the final chapter, although I have pointed to the key issues that really ought to be included in assignments in terms of wellbeing, vulnerability and life-chances it would be useful to consider how you might weave all of these together as an essay.

4 CONCLUSION: SO WHAT?

4.1 This book as an essay

I want to end this book by raising a question that you can often put to good use, so what? This is a question that you can always usefully apply to both what you have read and what you have written. So, having read a book or a journal article you should say so what? What does this mean or what can you do with it.

Let's start to think "so what" by encouraging you to think about how this book may contribute to the type of assignments that you will be required to submit as an undergraduate student within the UK. A lot of the time you will find that you are being asked to write essay type assignments. Very often you will be told that your work should be academic, or critical. To be both academic and critical I think that you should set out to make good use of books and articles which are written by academics and you should also question what you read. This means asking "so what", you always need to be avoiding describing what you have read about and be aiming to make sense of what you have read about. Think about how, in this book, I have provided a thread and how this could be read as an essay. Let's say I was given an essay title along the lines of "Critically explain wellbeing in relation to childhood".

So, the book started by discussing wellbeing, but it did it critically by noting that wellbeing is not something that we can take for granted. You should remember wellbeing being referred to as a slippery concept. Being able to demonstrate that you understand why it may be called a slippery concept, or why it might not be as straightforward as it first seems will always make you appear stronger. Of course, you then need to be able to support your claim and that is why you are always being asked to reference your work.

Students often get anxious about referencing but might that be because it is one of the few things in respect of social science at Higher Education that can be right or wrong? Your university will provide you with clear guidance as to how to reference but think about it as a way of relocating a book or journal article that you read. So, it's just like Hansel and Gretel dropping white stones as they went into the forest so they could find their way back. Your reference lets you find your way back to a useful book or journal article.

So, back to how we might see this book as an essay. Having discussed wellbeing and suggesting that it is something that is desirable in chapter 2 I then raised the idea that some children may not achieve it because they are vulnerable. Introducing vulnerability provides us with an opportunity to consider the place of children within society alongside the different everyday life experiences of children. So, this is another opportunity to develop an argument based upon what you read which lets you demonstrate that you understood what factors contribute to wellbeing or what might be an obstacle to achieving it.

Here again you could demonstrate criticality by exploring just what we mean by vulnerability and how it can be constructed. You would have an opportunity to talk about how discourse contributes to understanding children and young people and this provides an opportunity to bring some further academic ideas in by considering Foucault. Name dropping some key theorists is always good.

So, we could see an essay which is about wellbeing moving on to consider how some children and young people may be considered as being vulnerable and how this may prevent them from achieving wellbeing. However, you could now widen the discussion up and suggest that because it is often said that poverty makes children vulnerable then it is worthwhile to consider the social context of wellbeing and vulnerability by looking at life-chances. We want children to achieve wellbeing, but we know some won't and life-chances is an academic approach to understanding why. I hope this is making sense because if it is you should then see why it is that I felt justified in considering inequalities in the UK and how social and economic changes impact upon children and young people.

So, although your focus starts with what appears at first sight to be a basic concept that applies to children an academic approach to understanding this means that you have to make sense of a range of other issues or concepts which might not initially seem obvious. You get given a seemingly straightforward question and then you think about the range of issues that have been covered, or will be covered, in the module that you are studying and think about which of them apply to the issue that you intend to write about.

4.2 Further reading

This is one of a number of short books that aim to provide a critical and theoretical introduction to key issues relating to studying childhood, and associated courses such as Children, Young People and Families or courses linked to social work for example. It is aimed at those students within Higher Education who are currently working with children and/or young people, or those students in Higher Education who intend to work with children and/or young people. There are some who may still think that theory and practice are separate; that in the real world it is what we do that is important not the theory. This is not the case, that what we do, what you do, practice, is shaped by both theory and politics which is why theory and politics are covered throughout the book.

Think about how the book is structured so that it begins with some common, or taken for granted ideas about children. Given what I said in section 4.1 above this is an approach that you should often be able to take into your own assignments. For example, the idea that children are inherently vulnerable or that it is important to consider a child's wellbeing or work to achieve their potential. This feeds into considerations of life-chances and how this is considered with respect to children.

I could have gone on to conclude with a discussion of the way in which we see, or understand, children by introducing two very different ways of understanding children: as becomings, or as beings. I wanted to keep the book focused though. It was never intended to cover everything about childhood so the discussion of children as beings or becomings is commented on here but is discussed in much more depth in the book "Children, Families and the State". In this book the basic idea that children are seen in terms of what they will become forms the basis for a discussion of how this fits with discussions about failing families, children's freedoms and the way in which the State acts in relation to families and children.

The idea of children as becomings, that is, being seen in terms of their future could have fit with ideas about safeguarding but I decided to focus on safeguarding in "Resilience, Risk and Safeguarding". Just like your essays then I had to make decisions about what fits best where in respect of the stories that I wanted to tell. Once again though I will demonstrate a critical approach to these ideas and show that all are subject to social factors and social influences.

The final thing in this book then is something that some students overlook. Don't. What comes at the end is really useful when it comes to how you can demonstrate engagement with your studies and how it could support the things that you will write about. It is, of course the reference list. When I was a student, before computers and before the internet, finding books and journal articles was nowhere near as easy as it is now and my go-to source was always the reference list in the books and journal articles that I did get hold of. I always thought, "if it's good enough for the author, it's good enough for me!" My advice is to get hold of some of the sources that I have used and have a read. Some will be challenging but that is not a bad thing at all.

References

ALSTON, P. 2019. Visit to the United Kingdom of Great Britain and Northern Ireland: Report of the Special Rapporteur on extreme poverty and human rights. United Nations.

ANDERSON, D. L. & GRAHAM, A. P. 2016. Improving student wellbeing: having a say at school. *School Effectiveness & School Improvement.*

BECKER, S. 1997. *Responding to Poverty: The Politics of Cash and Care,* Harlow, Longman,.

BEN-ARIEH, A. 2006. Is the study of the "State of our children" changing? Re-visiting after 5 years. *Children and Youth Services Review,* 28, 799-812.

BRADSHAW, J. (ed.) 2016. *The well-being of children in the UK,* Bristol: Policy Press.

BRONFENBRENNER, U. 1979. *The ecology of human development: Experiments by nature and design,* Cambridge, MA, Harvard University Press.

BROTHERTON, G. & CRONIN, T. M. 2013. *Working with Vulnerable Children, Young People and Families*, London, Routledge.

BROWN, K. 2017. *Vulnerability and young people: care and social control in policy and practice,* Bristol, Policy Press.

CAIN, R. 2016. Responsibilising recovery: lone and low-paid parents, Universal Credit and the gendered contradictions of UK welfare reform. *British Politics,* 488.

CALDER, G. 2018. What Would a Society Look Like Where Children's Life Chances Were Really Fair? *Local Economy,* 33, 655-666.

CHILDREN'S SOCIETY, T. 2018. The Good Childhood Report 2018. London.

CHOONARA, J. 2019. *Insecurity, Precarious Work and Labour Markets: Challenging the Orthodoxy,* Cham, Springer International Publishing.

CHURCHILL, H. 2013. Retrenchment and restructuring: family support and children's services reform under the coalition. *Journal of Children's Services,* 8**,** 209-223.

CORAM & CORAM, I. 2017. Constructing a Definition of Vulnerability – Attempts to Define and Measure London.

CREASY, R. 2020. *Resilience, Risk and Safeguarding: A critical introduction for Childhood Studies*

CREASY, R. & CORBY, F. 2019. *Taming childhood?: a critical perspective on policy, practice and parenting,* Basingstoke, Hampshire, Palgrave Macmillan.

DICKERSON, A. & POPLI, G. 2018. The Many Dimensions of Child Poverty: Evidence from the UK Millennium Cohort Study*. *Fiscal Studies,* 39**,** 265.

ECCLESTONE, K. & HAYES, D. 2009. *The dangerous rise of therapeutic education,* London, Routledge.

FATTORE, T., MASON, J. & WATSON, E. 2007. Children's Conceptualisation(s) of Their Well-Being. *Social Indicators Research,* 80**,** 5.

FAVA, N. M., LI, T., BURKE, S. L. & WAGNER, E. F. 2017. Resilience in the context of fragility: Development of a multidimensional measure of child wellbeing within the Fragile Families dataset. *Children and Youth Services Review,* 81**,** 358-367.

FOUCAULT, M. 1989. *The birth of the clinic: an archaeology of medical perception,* London, Routledge.

FUREDI, F. 2004. *Therapy culture: cultivating vulnerability in an uncertain age,* London, Routledge.

GERRARD, J. 2017. *Precarious Enterprise on the Margins: Work, Poverty, and Homelessness in the City,* New York, Palgrave Macmillan US.

GILLBORN, D. & YOUDELL, D. 1999. *Rationing education : Policy, practice, reform and equity.,* Buckingham, Open University Press.

GROSS, S.-A., MUSGRAVE, G. & JANCIUTE, L. 2018. *Well-being and mental health in the gig economy: policy perspectives on precarity,* London, University of Westminster Press.

HIRSCH, D. 2018. The 'living wage' and low income: Can adequate pay contribute to adequate family living standards? *Critical Social Policy,* 38, 367-386.

JAMES, A. 2009. Childhood matters: Is children's wellbeing a high enough priority. *MENTAL HEALTH TODAY* 18-21.

JOHN, E. & FURNISH, D. 2017. Elton John 'We want to raise children who accept our choices'. *The Daily Telegraph.*

JONES, O. 2016. *Chavs: the demonization of the working class,* London, Verso.

JUPP, E. 2017. Families, policy and place in times of austerity. *Area,* 49, 266-273.

KNIGHT, A., LA PLACA, V. & MCNAUGHT, A. (eds.) 2014. *Wellbeing: policy and practice,* Banbury: Lantern.

LA PLACA, V. & KNIGHT, A. 2014. Wellbeing: A new policy phenomenon? *In:* MCNAUGHT, A., LA PLACA, V. & KNIGHT, A. (eds.) *Wellbeing: policy and practice.* Branbury, UK: Lantern Publishing Limited.

LAMBIE-MUMFORD, H. & GREEN, M. A. 2017. Austerity, welfare reform and the rising use of food banks by children in England and Wales. *Area,* 49, 273-280.

LAMBIE-MUMFORD, H. & GREEN, M. A. 2017. Austerity, welfare reform and the rising use of food banks by children in England and Wales. *Area,* 49, 273-279.

LAYARD, R. 2011. *Happiness: lessons from a new science,* London, Penguin.

LEHTONEN, A. 2018. 'Helping Workless Families': Cultural Poverty and the Family in Austerity and Anti-welfare Discourse. *Sociological Research Online,* 23, 84.

LEMOYNE, T. & BUCHANAN, T. 2011. Does 'hovering' matter? Helicopter parenting and its effects on well-beingG. *Sociological Spectrum.*

LYNDON, S. 2019. Troubling Discourses of Poverty in Early Childhood in the UK. *Children & Society,* 33, 602-609.

MARMOT, M. 2015. 'The richer you are, the better your health – and how this can be changed'. *The Guardian,* 11 September 2015.

MCELWEE, N. 2007. Chapter 1: Snowflake Children. *Child & Youth Services,* 29, 1-27.

MCNAMEE, S. 2016. *The Social study of Childhood,* London, Palgrave.

MCNAUGHT, A. 2011. Defining Wellbeing. *In:* KNIGHT, A. & MCNAUGHT, A. (eds.) *Understanding Wellbeing: An Introduction for Students and Practitioners of Health and Social Care.* Lantern Publishing.

MOORE, K. 2019. *Wellbeing and Aspirational Culture,* Cham, Springer International Publishing.

MUNRO, L. 2019. Life Chances, Education and Social Movements. London,: Anthem Press.

NICOLSON, P. 2014. *A critical approach to human growth and development,* Basingstoke, Palgrave Macmillan.

O'SULLIVAN, M., GUNNIGLE, P., TURNER, T., RYAN, L., MCMAHON, J., LAVELLE, J. & MURPHY, C. 2019. *Zero Hours and On-call Work in Anglo-Saxon Countries,* Singapore, Springer Singapore.

ONS 2018. Statistical bulletin: UK labour market: February 2018 Estimates of employment, unemployment, economic inactivity and other employment-related statistics for the UK. London: Office for National Statistics.

REAY, D., DAVID, M., E, & BALL, S. 2005. *Degrees of Choice: social class, race and gender in higher education,,* Stoke on Trent, Trentham Books.

REAY, D., DAVIES, J., DAVID, M. & BALL, S. J. 2001. Choices of Degree or Degrees of Choice? Class, `Race' and the Higher Education Choice Process. *Sociology,* 35, 855-874.

RIDGE, T. 2013. 'We are All in This Together'? The Hidden Costs of Poverty, Recession and Austerity Policies on Britain's Poorest Children. *Children & Society,* 27, 406-417.

ROBERTS, R. 2010. *Wellbeing from birth,* London, SAGE.

ROSE, W. & MCAULEY, C. 2019. Poverty and its impact on parenting in the UK: Re-defining the critical nature of the relationship through examining lived experiences in times of austerity. *Children and Youth Services Review,* 97, 134-141.

RYAN, F. 2019. Young people like Jess need the safety net. But austerity has destroyed it; Councils are buckling under the strain of families in crisis, thanks to catastrophic cuts to children and young people's services. *The Guardian (London, England)*, 2019/02/28/.

SIXSMITH, J., GABHAINN, S. N., FLEMING, C. & O'HIGGINS, S. 2007. Children's, Parents' and Teachers' Perceptions of Child Wellbeing. *Health Education,* 107, 511-524.

SMITH, M. J. 1998. *Social Science in Question* London, Sage.

SPRATT, J. 2016. Childhood wellbeing: what role for education? *British Educational Research Journal,* 42, 223-239.

TAYLOR, D. 2011. Wellbeing and Welfare: A Psychosocial Analysis of Being Well and Doing Well Enough. *JOURNAL OF SOCIAL POLICY,* 40, 777-795.

TUNSTILL, J. & WILLOW, C. 2017. Professional social work and the defence of children's and their families' rights in a period of austerity: A case study. *Social Work & Social Sciences Review.*

TURNBULL, G. 2016. The price of youth: commodification of young people through malleable risk practices. *Journal of Youth Studies,* 19, 1007-1022.

TURNBULL, G. & SPENCE, J. 2011. What's at risk? The proliferation of risk across child and youth policy in England. *JOURNAL OF YOUTH STUDIES,* 14, 939-960.

WELLARD, I. & SECKER, M. 2017. 'Visions' for children's health and wellbeing: exploring the complex and arbitrary processes of putting theory into practice. *Sport, Education and Society,* 22, 586-601.

WILKINSON, R. G. & PICKETT, K. 2010. *The spirit level: why equality is better for everyone,* London, Penguin.

WILKINSON, R. G. & PICKETT, K. 2018. *The Inner Level: How More Equal Societies Reduce Stress, Restore Sanity and Improve Everyone's Wellbeing,* London, Allen Lane.

INDEX

Aimhigher 30
Aspiration 29-30
Austerity 6, 8

Child Poverty Act 2010 23
      Life-chances Act 2010, 23

Discourse 12-13
Discrimination 26-27

Equal Pay legislation 25-26, 28
Food banks 32
Foucault 2, 12
Functionalism 31

Gender inequality 29
Gig economy 6, 22

Happiness 7
Hardworking families 15
Health 2-3
Helicopter parenting 5
Higher Education 30

Life-chances 22, 24, 35, 37, 41
      Life-chances Act 2010 23
Life-choices 27-28, 37

Mental health 7-8

Needs 13-15

Neoliberalism   6

Potential   29
Poverty   16, 23, 33-36, 40

Referencing   40
Risk   20

Sheffield Wednesday FC,   25
Snowflakes   18-19

Vulnerable   10, 12-20, 25, 40

Welfare Reform and Work Act 2016   23
Wellbeing   1-10, 25, 39
        Subjective wellbeing   3, 10

ABOUT THE AUTHOR

Dr Rob Creasy was previously Director of Social Sciences at York St John University in the UK. He has taught in Further Education and Higher Education for over 30 years. He is the author of "The Taming of Education" (2018) published by Palgrave Macmillan and the co-author of "Taming Childhood" (2019) also published by Palgrave Macmillan as well as a number of journal articles. He wasn't all that good at school and got his first "O" level aged 25. His undergraduate and postgraduate degrees are in Sociology, Social Policy and Education and he is a Senior Fellow of the Higher Education Academy. In 2015 he led on the introduction of BA Sociology at York St John University, in 2019 this was ranked as the number 1 sociology course in the UK based on student satisfaction as reported in the National Student Satisfaction survey.

Finally

Many thanks for reading this, you are welcome to provide feedback and/or suggestions via my email address:

robcreasy@hotmail.co.uk

If you do want to get in touch you might provide a brief response to the following questions:

- Overall, was it useful? Is there anything that I should add or change?
- Have I got the tone right, is it too theoretical or not theoretical enough? Does it make sense to you?

I do have a favour to ask though. I decided to self-publish this book because the prices that major publishers charge can be prohibitive. By self-publishing I can sell this, and other related books as referred to, for a relatively small amount but that means that I don't have a marketing budget. So, two things will really help me:

1. Please recommend this book to friends;
2. Please leave a review on Amazon, having lots of reviews is really helpful.

Best wishes, Rob.

Printed in Great Britain
by Amazon